Con[tents]

Mr & Mrs William Proby & Family

History of The Family

Almost since the time of the Norman Conquest there has been a house where Elton Hall now stands. The present owners, the Proby family who originally came from Chester, have owned land at Elton for 400 years. Previously, from 1450-1600, it was the residence of the Sapcotes, who built the 15th-century tower which still survives and bears their coat of arms. Prior to that the history is more obscure but it is likely that the de Aylingtons had a moated house on the site.

The connection of the Proby family with Elton dates from the 16th century when Sir Peter Proby, who held various high offices in the reign of Queen Elizabeth I and King James I and who subsequently in 1622 became Lord Mayor of London, was granted a Crown lease of the Elton watermills by Elizabeth in 1596. However, it was not until his grandson, Sir Thomas Proby (1634-1689) married the daughter of a wealthy local landowner, Sir Thomas Cotton, who brought with her the site of the present Hall, that the Proby family built a residence at Elton in 1666.

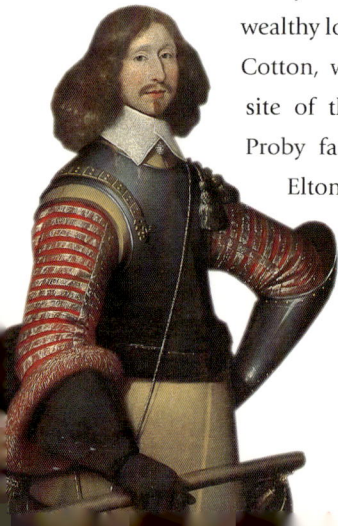

Sir Thomas Proby
(1634-1689)

Sir Thomas Proby led an active life as a country gentleman and Member of Parliament for Huntingdon. His account books reveal him to be a methodical and conscientious landlord. From Sir Thomas, the Hall passed first to his brother John and then through their uncle to William Proby, a cousin of Sir Thomas and great grandson of Sir Peter Proby. William Proby was a member of the East India Company and Governor of Fort St. George, Madras. William Proby's grandson, John Proby, succeeded to the Hall in 1760.

In 1750 John Proby had married the Irish heiress, Elizabeth Allen, elder daughter of the 2nd Viscount Allen, and sister of the 3rd Viscount who was killed in a street brawl in 1745. Through his wife, John Proby acquired large estates in Ireland and Stillorgan House on the south side of Dublin. Within two years of his marriage, John Proby was created Baron Carysfort in the peerage of Ireland, taking his title from an Allen property in County Wicklow.

John Proby
1st Lord,
Carysfort
by Reynolds

2

His son John Joshua Proby, succeeded him in 1772. John Joshua's second wife whom he married in 1787, was Elizabeth Grenville, sister of William Grenville (created Baron Grenville in 1790) Prime Minister from 1806-1807. Elizabeth was the daughter of George Grenville whose sister was married to William Pitt and her elder brother became the 1st Marquis of Buckingham. John Joshua was MP for Stamford from 1790 onwards and between 1800-1802 became Ambassador to Berlin and Special Emissary to the Imperial Court in Russia. He was created Earl of Carysfort in 1789 and in 1801 was given a United Kingdom barony, enabling him to sit in the House of Lords. On the formation of The Ministry of all the Talents formed by his brother-in-law Lord Grenville in 1806, he became a member of the Privy Council and was appointed joint Post-Master General. He resigned all his posts when the Duke of Portland acceded to power in Spring 1807. He died in 1828 and was succeeded by two of his sons who became the 2nd and 3rd Earl respectively.

The 5th and last Earl of Carysfort

The 5th and last Earl of Carysfort inherited Elton Hall on the death of his brother, the 4th Earl in 1872. The 5th Earl died in 1909 and Elton Hall then passed through the last Earl's sister to the current occupant, William Proby, who is the great, great (times 10) grandson of Sir Peter Proby. Sir Richard Proby (1886-1979) was created a baronet in 1952 for services to agriculture and politics, thus restoring the baronetcy to the family. The current baronet, Sir Peter Proby, father of William Proby, was Lord Lieutenant for Cambridgeshire.

Master (the future 1st Earl of Carysfort) and Miss Proby by Reynolds

Elizabeth Osborne, 1st wife of 1st Earl of Carysfort by Romney

3

The History of the House

The Hall is a mixture of styles. The garden or south front incorporates the 15th century tower and chapel which were built by the Sapcotes at the time of Henry VII. There was probably a medieval house as well, none of which remains. When Sir Thomas Proby acquired the house in the middle of the 17th century, it was in a very run down state of repair. He built a new reversed L shaped house with the north end prolonged westward as a wing and this, together with the tower and chapel, is shown in Bucks' view circa 1730.

Bridges, in his *History of Northamptonshire* in 1720 describes Elton as follows: "In the old part of the house still remaining is this chapel, having on each side of the altar a niche for a statue of a large size. The ceiling and gallery are of old oak wainscot." It is not clear who was responsible for filling in the angle at the side of Sir Thomas's building and joining the restoration house onto the medieval chapel. It could have been Sir Thomas himself or his brother John who succeeded him in 1689 or his cousin, William Proby who inherited in 1710. The same person would have probably also been responsible for adding the Octagon rooms and beyond on the south side of the house whose foundations can only be given a rough date of between the late seventeenth or early eighteenth century. It is also possible that the chapel was converted for some alternative use at this time since in Bucks' view the east window has been filled in.

Little else seems to have been done to the house until his grandson John, (1st Lord Carysfort), became involved from 1750 onwards. It is not certain whether John or his father was the instigator for fully converting the medieval chapel into the Drawing Room, but it can be dated to 1750-60 by the decoration of the ceiling and the chimneypiece (which was moved to the Dining Room in 1860: the Carysfort cypher now incorporated into the chimneypiece was added then). The wide bay window on the south front was probably formed at the same time. The 1st Lord who finally inherited the Hall in 1760 was also responsible for the rococo chimneypiece in the Lower Octagon Room.

His son, who became the 1st Earl, succeeded in 1772 and was seldom out of the builders' hands until his death in 1828. He began by consulting John Carter, the antiquary and draughtsman of Gothic buildings, but later on became his own architect. Carter was probably responsible for the Gothic decoration of the Upper Octagon Room and might have suggested the Gothic facing to the south front to the west of the chapel. The end of this range has two round towers which were built between 1812 and 1814

4

Bucks' view of Sir Thomas Proby's house c. 1730

and it is known that French prisoners of war from the prison camp at Norman Cross worked extensively on the house. The gatehouse was joined to the rest of the house with a two-storey block and the upper room of this block which is now the Library, has a Jacobean mullioned bay window which came from a house owned by the Drydens in neighbouring Chesterton. Also at this time, the whole of Sir Thomas Proby's dwelling was faced with stucco and given a highly castellated appearance. To save expense, the battlements and turret tops were made of wood and painted to look like stone. The appearance of the house after these drastic alterations is recorded in a series of drawings made in 1850.

Much of this work was undone by the 3rd Earl of Carysfort when he succeeded in 1855. As his architect, he engaged Henry Ashton who had worked under Wyatville at Windsor. A lot of the Gothic trimmings were removed and a classic style reverting some distance towards the original treatment of Sir Thomas Proby's building was adopted. In 1860, the 3rd Earl was also responsible for adding the Dining Rooms to the north side

of the medieval chapel and embellishing the Marble Hall which joins together the disparate parts of the house. The south front, however, still retained much of the Gothic appearance but with the addition of an extra storey behind the Upper Octagon Room to house the Marble Hall, and another tower which was added to the east of it in 1870 by the 4th Earl. Between 1868-1872 the 4th Earl also built a Billiard Room and new kitchen on the east side of the gatehouse. He also added a new stable block onto the early 18th century yard. In 1882 the 5th Earl took down the first Gothic tower straddling the west and southern fronts behind the stepped gable. The design of the tower had always been attributed to Batty Langley (1696-1751) but the date of the building was probably during the 1st Earl's lifetime. The second stepped gable behind the first one and the adjoining battlements were then built to harmonise. Little has been done since then but the present occupant, William Proby, also feels that he is rarely out of the builders' hands, this time for restoration rather than grand Gothick plans.

The Steward's Room

In the 1860s two dining rooms were built on the north side of the drawing room. Originally, the Kitchen was situated under the Dining Room. At the end of the 19th century new servants' quarters were formed under the dining rooms, the Steward's Room being one of these. The kitchens were moved to the far side of the small courtyard – where the State Coach is now housed – and food was carried through a covered way to dining rooms above.

The Steward's Room was used by the Steward or Butler to the household and other senior servants. At meal-times in many country houses it was the practice for senior servants to eat only the meat course with all the indoor staff and then retire to the Steward's Room for pudding. The Steward or Butler would also entertain the servants of any visitors to the house. Strict rules of etiquette applied to the treatment of these visiting staff depending on the rank of their employer.

Besides providing a welcome to visitors to the Hall there are many items on display that relate to life on the estate and in the house.

In the Museum room beyond there is a detailed history of the family and house together with a changing exhibition of some of the rare books in the library.

Dress sword of Midshipman Proby, afterwards 3rd Earl of Carysfort

The Carysfort State Coach

6

The Chapel

Fan vaulting in the Chapel

19th century copy of a della Robbia terracotta
and enamel plaque

This room was not originally the Chapel but was converted after the last war. It was formed from part of the undercroft of the Sapcotes' Chapel and the vaulting is late 15th-century. It is still used as a Church of England Chapel and family Christenings take place here.

From the Chapel, a door leads to the Lower Octagon Room.

7

Lower Octagon Room

Eastward Ho! by Henry O'Neil

This room mirrors the design in the Upper Octagon Room immediately above it. The room features many beautiful and important works of art, not least Henry O'Neil's (1817-1880) celebrated *Eastward Ho!* (*pictured above*), which shows British soldiers departing to quell the Indian Mutiny in 1857. Below the picture is a marble side table supported by a large gilt eagle with 19th century giltwood framed music chairs upholstered in Beauvais tapestry.

The Evening of Life by Théophile Lybaert
(b. 1848)

Engravings of London Life
by Wilkie

A dedication to Bacchus by Sir Lawrence Alma Tadema (1836-1912)

*The Marble Hall with a white marble statue of Esmeralda by
Romanelli (1868). On the wall behind to the left is the seascape
"And There is Never Silence on That Shore"
by Peter Graham (1903). To the left is a 19th century bust of
Lord Grenville, Prime Minister 1806-1807*

*At the top of the stairs is
a Roman bust of Lucius Verus*

Marble Hall

The Marble Hall and main staircase designed by Ashton are remarkable examples of a mid-Victorian revival of mid-18th-century style. The large clock under the gallery is an *Act of Parliament* clock. The portraits on either side of the central doorway are of the last Earl and Countess of Carysfort. The last Earl collected many of the best paintings, furniture and books in the house. He succeeded in restoring to the house the quality of the very fine collection built by the 1st Earl of Carysfort which had been sold in 1828. The painting hanging on the right hand wall above the door is of Sir Thomas Proby (died 1689) who was the first member of the Proby family to make Elton Hall his home.

Charlotte Heathcote, wife of the 5th Earl by Millais (1829-1896)

18th century German Boulle clock with an English mechanism

11

Yellow Drawing Room

The Yellow Drawing Room with a mid-eighteenth century fireplace appears 18th-century in design, but more probably is the work of Henry Ashton, the 3rd Earl's architect. At the far end is an imposing pair of scagliola columns on each side of the entrance to the panelled hall. A pair of very fine English commodes are placed each side of the fireplace. Either side of the door, is a magnificent pair of cabinets which were made up for William Beckford, the builder of Fonthill Abbey and a famous and eccentric 18th-century collector. The cabinets are constructed from a 17th-century Japanese lacquer box, probably acquired by the wife of the Governor of the Dutch East India Company between 1635-39. They were made under the direction of the firm of Vulliamy in 1803. The firm used many distinguished craftsmen of the day and probably as many as thirty people worked on an important commission such as this. The main designer was Henri Auguste, the foremost Parisian goldsmith of the 1790s.

George III bois - clair commode

*Stillorgan House and Park,
home of the Allen family,
by Dominique Serres, 1722-1793*

The charming painting over the fireplace *(see detail opposite)* is by Millais and called *The Minuet*. The model was Millais's daughter, Effie, although it is thought that he used an older model for the arms of the child. The chair in the painting is known to have belonged to Thackeray and was borrowed by Millais for the occasion.

After the Yellow Drawing Room the Marble Hall staircase leads to the Upper Octagon Room.

*William Beckford
and the Cabinet once
owned by him*

Upper Octagon Room

The Great Seal of Queen Elizabeth I
attached to the Crown Lease of
Elton Mill given to Sir Peter Proby in 1596

Sèvres plate, part of the dinner service belonging to Catherine the Great of Russia

Vincennes tureen and cover

Miniatures of the 3rd Earl and his wife. The delicately plaited locks of hair spell out the initials I.P. & G.P.; Isabella Proby and Granville Proby

The room dates in its present form from the end of the 18th century and appears now much as it did in the drawing (on show in the Drawing Room) made by William Wells in 1818. The gilding was added in 1860 when the room was redecorated together with the Drawing Room. The stained glass window is dated 1783 and shows the Proby coat of arms and coronet. John Carter was probably responsible for the Gothic design of this room although the Gothic style glass cabinets were added later for the display of the fine collection of Sèvres china. Of particular note are the two plates at the top of the display cabinet on the right of the window, which belonged to Catherine the Great of Russia (1778).

The display cabinet in the centre of the room contains various articles of interest connected with the family. Of particular note is the Seal of Elizabeth I on the grant of Elton Mill to Sir Peter Proby in 1596.

The cabinet opposite the window is 16th-century Italian. It came from the Duke of Hamilton's collection at Hamilton Palace and was formerly in the collection of William Beckford of Fonthill. The firescreen is made up with Beauvais tapestry and matches the set of furniture in the Drawing Room.

Drawing Room

The room in 1818
when used as a library,
painted by
Captain William Wells

1st Earl of Carysfort
by Sir Joshua Reynolds
(1723-1792)

The Drawing Room is the largest room in the house and was formed from the medieval Chapel in about 1760. The 18th-century ceiling with its enriched cornice and frieze remains, but the present decoration dates from 1860.

Most of the paintings are of the family and by Sir Joshua Reynolds. He was a friend of the 1st Lord Carysfort and it is believed that he stayed at the Hall. Immediately on the right after entering the Drawing Room is a drawing which is a self-portrait by Reynolds. On the left is a small picture painted in 1818 by Captain William Wells, who was married to Lady Elizabeth, daughter of the 1st Earl of Carysfort. This shows what the room was like at that time, when it was used as a library.

Louis XVI
gilt-framed chair with
Beauvais Tapestry

Self portrait by Sir Joshua Reynolds

The Snake in the Grass by Sir Joshua Reynolds

As you enter the room there is a table which is an exact replica of the one Marie Antoinette had at the Petit Trianon. The original is still on show at Versailles.

Most of the furniture in the Drawing Room is French. Of special interest is a suite of Louis XVI gilt-framed furniture. The seats and backs are upholstered in Beauvais tapestry designed with scenes from La Fontaine's fables after Oudry. Either side of the fireplace is a pair of 18th-century Boulle cabinets from the collection of Lord Whitworth. The painting on the far right on the wall facing the garden is Reynolds' *The Snake in the Grass*. Several versions of the

One of a pair of Louis XVI Boulle cabinets.

painting were done and the original Elton picture was sold in 1828 and is now in the Tate Gallery. This version was bought in 1909 from the Cuthbertson sale.

Immediately on the left of the bay window leading to the garden is a charming unfinished portrait of Kitty Fisher *(pictured below)* by Reynolds. Kitty Fisher was a famous courtesan known for her wit and beauty. In Victorian times, this painting was banished to the Housekeeper's Room as it was not considered suitable for lady members of the family to view.

Kitty Fisher by Reynolds

Charles Proby, Commissioner of Chatham Dockyard by Sir Joshua Reynolds

19

Dedham Vale by John Constable 1776-1837

Two close-up details showing Constable's masterly techniques in oils

Ante Dining Room

The Ante Dining Room was used for family meals when there were no guests present. The landscape by John Constable, shows a view of Dedham Vale and was painted in 1811. The other fine landscape in this room is after Gainsborough. The portrait above the door is by Gainsborough and is of John Proby, M.P., father of the 1st Lord Carysfort. The portrait over the fireplace is of John Proby by Kneller. He was the second son of Sir Heneage Proby and brother to Sir Thomas Proby.

The china in the display cabinets is part of a large dinner-service of Chinese *famille rose* armorial porcelain which was made in 1723. The custom at that time was to have a dinner-service made in China since the Chinese craftsmen were recognised masters of this art. In many cases, it could take as long as two years to order and deliver such services.

Two details from a plate from the early 18th century Yongzheng dinner service bearing the Proby Arms

Dining Room

Dining Room

This room was built in 1860 by the 3rd Earl of Carysfort and was designed by his architect, Henry Ashton. It was built immediately to the North of the medieval Chapel (now the Drawing Room) and the three large Gothic windows are exact copies of the windows that were in the North wall of the Chapel. The very fine fireplace is original 18th-century and was moved from the Drawing Room. The whole effect is very much of the 18th-century grand saloon. The County boundary used to run through the middle of this room and consequently gave rise to the remark that the Earl and Countess of Carysfort dined in separate counties.

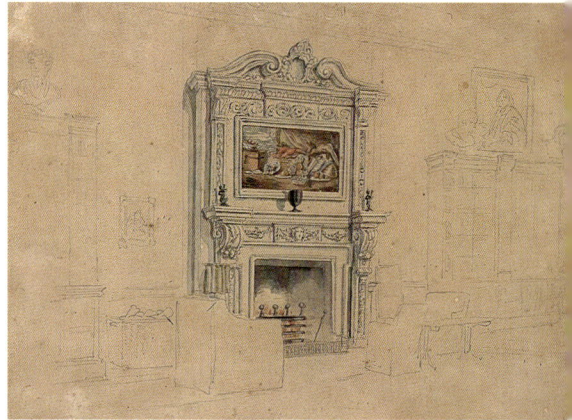

Drawing of the 18th century fireplace by the architect Henry Ashton (1860)

The Madonna of the Bas-Relief by Caesare da Sesto

The room was completely redecorated in 1983 and the pictures rehung in the 18th century manner, to show at its best the very good collection of old Masters and early portraits. A complete list of paintings in the room is available on the hand cards in the room. Of particular importance is the *Virgin of Mercy* by Girolamo Genga to the

24

right of the fireplace. By legend, this painting depicts the Blessed Virgin shielding with her mantle, nuns and monks of the Cistercian Order. To the left of the fireplace is a landscape by Hobbema and there is another fine landscape by Gaspar Dughet (called Poussin) on the right of the far wall. Two small paintings on the wall to the left of the doorway into the Ante Dining Room are of particular interest. Gerard Dow's *The Flute Player* is thought to be a self-portrait and is remarkable for the minute detail of the contents of the room in

The Flute Player by Gerard Dow

Landscape by Hobbema

which the figure is seated. Immediately to the left of the doorway is a small painting by Luini which represents a boy holding a pair of wooden tablets which, through an ingenious arrangement of straps, can be opened on both sides. It was painted at the beginning of the 16th century. Luini was a follower of Leonardo da Vinci and at one time this painting was attributed to him.

25

19th century marble bust of Lord Claud Hamilton husband of
Lady Elizabeth Proby. Their son, Douglas Hamilton
changed his name to Proby in 1904 in order to inherit

26

The Library

The Library contains a large collection of books, around 12,000 in number, and is one of the finest private collections in the country. It represents a continuous interest from the time of Sir Thomas Proby onwards. Unfortunately, a serious fire broke out in 1894 causing the destruction of a number of books and damage to many more. However, with the insurance money obtained, the 5th Earl was able to make a number of important purchases. Sadly, one such book, a Gutenberg bible, was sold in 1909 to pay death duties, but even so, the Library still contains many superb examples. Outstanding are the manuscripts, liturgical books and bibles.

The small cabinet beside the door on the left of the window contains Henry VIII's Prayer Book which includes writings by Henry VIII, Catherine Parr, her 3rd husband Thomas Seymour, Princess (afterwards Queen) Mary and Edward VI. The clock on the mantelpiece is nineteenth century English Boulle.

Henry VIII's Prayer Book

Inner Library

From the Main Library a short passage leads to the Inner Library which is situated in the Medieval Sapcote Tower. There is a small side room immediately on the right on entering the Inner Library, which looks out over the garden. The bust of the old man in the window is that of a gardener who, for nearly 70 years, tended the gravel paths in the gardens and park. A false door to the left of the window facing over the park leads to the top of the Tower.

On display in the Inner Library is Sir Thomas Proby's account book (illustrated opposite), and the list of salaries of the Court of Queen Elizabeth I. Sir Thomas Proby maintained meticulous accounts of all his expenditure, including the cost of the work done on converting the largely ruined dwelling into his home. He also appears to have been something of a gambler, as there are numerous entries to, 'lost at cards'.

Appeal for the Release of Monsieur Pierre de Bresze
Written by George Chastelain 1401

List of the Salaries paid at the Court of Elizabeth I
when Sir Peter Proby was Comptroller of the Household

The Grounds

Elton Hall sits in 200 acres of parkland bound by the river Nene on the western boundary. At one time during the eighteenth and nineteenth centuries the drive ran through the park to the neighbouring village of Warmington. There is supposedly a ghostly figure who appears by the small clump of trees close to the house. The ghost is said to be Robert Sapcote who did not like losing at cards and robbed his guests on their way home if he had lost too much money.

Very little evidence remains of what was the original garden. We can see from the 1730 Bucks' drawing of Sir Thomas Proby's house that a formal garden was laid out to the north-east of the house. Before that we can only presume that there was a moat round the Tudor tower and chapel. We have some sketches of what the grounds looked like in the mid to late eighteenth century, but it was very much lawn, trees and a few shrubs. Formal gardens and pleasure grounds were laid out in the 1890s by Edward Milner and

The new Orangery

The front of Elton Hall in Spring-time

in 1913 by Col. Douglas Proby to designs by his daughter-in-law's father, A.H. Hallam Murray. All that remains from the early planting is some of the mature trees and from the 1890s planting, the box parterre and four conical yew shapes on the south side of the house. The main structure of the gardens as you see them today, that is the paths, lawn, lily pond, well-head and rose garden wall, were constructed in 1913. The rest of Murray's planting which included the rose garden and bowling green together with the 1890s planting of a geometric pattern of yew on the main lawn and many mature elm trees, had all been lost by 1979. The new structure of hedges, lime and box avenues, gates, orangery, rose and shrub gardens have all been laid out since 1983 under the guidance of Meredyth Proby.

32